"The Greatest Invention in the History of Mankind Is Beer"

*and Other Manly Insights
from*
Dave Barry

D0108297

"The Greatest Invention in the History of Mankind Is Beer"

and Other Manly Insights
from
Dave Barry

**Andrews McMeel
Publishing**

Kansas City

ISBN: 0-7407-1525-9

Library of Congress Catalog Card Number: 00-108467

Book design by Lisa Martin
Illustrations by Matthew Taylor

Why do guys do macho things? One possible explanation is that they believe women are impressed. In fact, however, most women have the opposite reaction to macho behavior. You rarely hear women say things like, "Norm, when that vending machine failed to give you a Three Musketeers bar and you punched it so hard that you broke your hand and we had to go to the hospital instead of to my best friend's daughter's wedding, I became so filled with lust for you that I nearly tore off all my clothes right there in the emergency room." No, women are far more likely to say, "Norm, you have the brains of an Odor Eater."

1

Most TV beer commercials have the same plot: Some guys open some beers, and instantly the commercial is overrun by friendly seminaked young women resembling Barbie but taller and less intellectual. If you just got here from Mars, you wouldn't know, from watching these commercials, that beer is meant for internal consumption. You'd think it was a chemical Hot Babe Attractant, similar to what moths use to locate each other so they can mate.

Most males here on Earth do not do any more laundry than they absolutely have to. A single-sock load would not be out of the question for a guy. A guy might well choose to wash *only the really dirty part of the sock.*

My car has been named something like Rugged Macho Stud Hombre Four-by-Four of the Century by an outfit with a name like Magazine Writers Who Do Not Personally Own This Type of Car but Get to Drive New Ones for Free. My car needs to be rugged, because it takes a constant daily pounding from the tow truck dragging it back to the Mechanic Who Never Actually Fixes the Problem.

• • •

I like beer. On occasion I will even drink a beer to celebrate a major event such as the fall of communism or the fact that our refrigerator is still working.

Basic Guy
Fashion Rule

If, when you appear at the breakfast
table, your wife laughs so hard
that she spits out her toast,
you should consider wearing
a different tie.

The commitment problem has caused many women to mistakenly conclude that men, as a group, have the emotional maturity of hamsters. This is not the case. A hamster is *much* more capable of making a lasting commitment to a woman, especially if she gives it those little food pellets. Whereas a guy, in a relationship, will consume the pellets of companionship, and he will run on the exercise wheel of lust, but as soon as he senses that the door of commitment is about to close and trap him in the wire cage of true intimacy, he'll squirm out, scamper across the kitchen floor of uncertainty, and hide under the refrigerator of nonreadiness.

The most sensible way to ask a girl out is to walk directly up to her on foot and say, "So, you want to go out? Or what?" I never did this. I knew that there was always the possibility that the girl would say no, thereby leaving me with no viable option but to leave Harold C. Crittenden Junior High School forever and go into the woods and become a bark-eating hermit whose only companions would be the gentle and understanding woodland creatures.

"Hey, ZITFACE!" the woodland creatures would shriek in cute little Chip 'n' Dale voices while raining acorns down upon my head. "You wanna DATE? HAHAHAHAHAHA."

In college, I played in a rock band whose major musical credential was printed business cards. We felt that it was artistically important to have long, straight hair, so that when we got to the climactic part of "Twist and Shout," where the lyrics are, quote, *ah, ahh, ahhh, ahhh, AHHHHHHHH Shake it up BABY now,* we could whip our hair around our faces in a dramatic fashion to indicate deep emotion.

8

I think the Men's Movement is a fine idea. I'm definitely out of touch with my own masculinity, a fact that was driven home when our bathroom ceiling collapsed. A virile man would have known how to fix it. But I am totally out of touch with my masculine nature, so all I could do was call a plumber. He went into the attic and, following his natural masculine instinct, knew immediately what to do: Call for more plumbers. Soon there was a whole tribal gathering up there, virile men who were not afraid to crawl around the attic and confront naked plumbing and shout and roar and pound on things. They might also have been hugging. I stayed downstairs, making coffee and keeping the checkbook warm.

Most American guys are reluctant to use fragrances on the theory that if you start wearing perfume, you're heading down a slippery slope that will inevitably lead to rouge, leotards, watching *Oprah,* etc. So most guys prefer to emit only natural male aromas such as B.O. and ketchup.

• • •

I hate to engage in gender stereotyping, but when women plan the menu for a recreational outing, they usually come up with a nutritionally balanced menu featuring all the major food groups, including the Sliced Carrots Group, the Pieces of Fruit Cut into Cubes Group, the Utensils Group, and the Plate Group. Whereas guys tend to focus on the Carbonated Malt Beverages Group and the Fatal Snacks Group.

The fundamental question: How can a guy say he's "not ready" to make a permanent commitment to a woman with whom he is obviously compatible; a woman with whom he has been intimate for years; a woman who once drove *his* dog to the veterinarian in *her* new car when it (the dog) started regurgitating violently after eating an entire birthday cake, including candles, that *she* made from scratch for *him* (the guy), the result being that her car will smell like a stadium rest room for the next five years, at the end of which this guy will probably *still* say he's "not ready"?

Why is it that a woman will forgive homicidal behavior in a horse, yet be highly critical of a man for leaving the toilet seat up?

Examples of pointlessly destructive or hurtful macho guy behavior include:

- Guys at sporting events getting into shoving matches and occasionally sustaining fatal heart attacks over such issues as who was next in line for pretzels.

- Guys on the street making mouth noises at women.

- Boxing.

- Foreign policy.

Steroids, as you know, are substances that some guys put in their bodies in an effort to develop bulging, rippling, sharply defined muscles like the ones Michael Keaton wore in *Batman*. This is foolish, because women are not attracted to rippling, sharply defined muscles. Women prefer a type of male physique that is known, in body-building circles, as "the newspaper columnist."

Gary told Suzanne that he felt—this is classic guy thinking—they should either break up or get married, and naturally, being "not ready," he stopped seeing her. Suzanne writes, "I don't understand why some men seem to have more access to automatic teller machines than to their own emotions. Gary reads your column, so could you please write a piece about the myth of 'hearing bells' or why guys hate to give up their freedom or how some guys wouldn't know a good wife if she hit him on the head with her diaphragm."

• • •

Guys are born with a fundamental, genetically transmitted mental condition known to psychologists as the Fear That if You Get Married, Some Single Guy, Somewhere, Will Be Having More Fun Than You.

The deeply moving picture *Field of Dreams* tells the heartwarming story of a man, played by Kevin Costner, who receives instruction from corn. One day the corn tells him to build a baseball field next to his house, so naturally he does. (It could have been worse: A really malevolent vegetable, such as zucchini, would have told him to build a nuclear reactor.)

Watching *Field of Dreams,* especially the emotion-packed ending, I had tears in my eyes as I thought to myself: *How come my wife never looks at me the way she looks at Kevin Costner?*

The most important Fashion Rule that has been drummed into guys is *Never wear a brown suit.* Only two kinds of guys wear brown suits:

1. Your Uncle Wally, the retired accordion broker who attends all family functions—weddings, funerals, picnics—wearing a brown suit that he purchased during the Truman administration and that he has never had cleaned or repaired, despite the fact that the pants have a large devastated region resulting from the time in 1974 when he fell asleep with his cigar burning and set fire to his crotch and Aunt Louise had to extinguish it with egg nog.

2. Ronald Reagan.

Steroids can cause men to develop *thick Austrian accents.* This is what happened to Arnold Schwarzenegger, who was actually born and raised in Topeka, Kansas, and spoke like a regular American until he used steroids to build his body up to the point where he was legally classified by the U.S. Census Bureau as "construction equipment."

• • •

In small quantities, testosterone produces only mild side effects, such as the inability to stop pressing the channel-changing button on the TV remote control. But at higher levels, testosterone causes destructive male behavior, the two most terrible kinds being:

1. War.
2. Do-it-yourself projects.

Oh, they don't *call* it perfume. They call it "fragrance for men," and they give it guy-type names like "El Hombre de Male Man for Him," but it's definitely perfume. This is alarming to me because I grew up in an environment where, if you had shown up at school wearing a fragrance, the other males would have stuffed you into a gym locker and left you there for the better part of the academic year.

• • •

It's a well-known fact that a male with even a moderate testosterone level would rather drill a hole in his hand (which he probably will) than admit, especially to his spouse, that he cannot do something himself.

Many men are *afraid* to do laundry, especially laundry belonging to people of other genders, because they (the males) might get into Big Trouble. I know I would. In our household we have a lot of sensitive garments with laundering-instruction tags full of strict instructions like:

DO NOT MACHINE-WASH.

DO NOT USE BLEACH.

DO NOT USE WARM WATER.

DO NOT USE ANY WATER.

DO NOT TOUCH THIS GARMENT
WITHOUT SURGICAL GLOVES.

PUT THIS GARMENT DOWN IMMEDIATELY,
YOU CLUMSY OAF.

Married guys assume that unmarried guys lead lives of constant excitement involving Jacuzzis full of international fashion models, whereas in fact for most unmarried guys the climax of the typical evening is watching *America's Most Alarming Criminals* while eating onion dip straight from the container. This is also true of *married* guys, but statistically they are far more likely to be using a spoon.

• • •

Put an ordinary male on the Space Shuttle, and within minutes he'll be telling his spouse that by God he'll repair the retro thruster modules, because if you call in NASA they'll just charge you an arm and a leg.

personally have destroyed numerous perfectly good rooms by undertaking frenzied testosterone-induced efforts to fix them up despite the fact that I have the manual dexterity of an oyster. Hundreds of years from now, archaeologists will look at my home-improvement projects and say, "This civilization was apparently wiped out by a terrible natural disaster involving spackle."

developed my laundering skills in college, where I used what laundry scientists call the Pile System, wherein you put your dirty undershorts on the floor until they form a waist-high pile, thus subjecting the bottom shorts to intense heat and pressure that causes them to become, over several months, clean enough to wear if you're desperate and spray them with Right Guard brand deodorant.

You can be exposed to male fragrances *against your will* merely by exercising your constitutional right to leaf through magazines. For example, while leafing through *GQ* I was attacked by an aggressive Calvin Klein male-fragrance advertisement that deliberately spewed fragrance molecules onto my body, and for several hours I was terrified that I might have to make a trip to a masculine environment such as the hardware store for an emergency toilet part or something, and the clerks would pick up my scent:

Clerk (sniffing): Smells like a moose conflated in here! Is that *you*?

Maybe you've heard about the Men's Movement. It consists of men who feel they've lost touch with their fundamental masculinity because of the restrictive pressures of the modern world, with its industrialization, neckties, fireworks regulations, etc. So these men are forming groups that only men can belong to, similar to the U.S. Senate, except that they engage in virile ritualistic male-bonding behavior such as shouting and roaring and hugging and pounding on drums. I'm not making this movement up. It was on the cover of *Newsweek,* so you know it's not just a passing fad. It's a fad that will probably be around for *months.*

The fragrance industry has for years been running an advertising campaign based on the theme that a fragrance-wearing guy will need a fully charged cattle prod to fend off seminaked women. You've seen the magazine ads, which usually feature a guy being stared at by a woman whose facial expression says, "I am receiving your fragrance! Let's have carnal relations right here in the magazine!"

The first rule of dating: Never risk direct contact with the girl in question. Your role model should be the nuclear submarine, gliding silently beneath the ocean surface, tracking an enemy target that does not even begin to suspect that the submarine would like to date it. I spent the vast majority of 1960 keeping a girl named Judy under surveillance, maintaining a minimum locker distance of fifty lockers to avoid the danger that I might somehow get into a conversation with her, which could have led to disaster:

Judy: Hi.

Me: Hi.

Judy: Just in case you have ever thought about having a date with me, the answer is no.

Without question, the greatest invention in the history of mankind is beer.

Oh, I grant you that the wheel was also a fine invention, but the wheel does not go nearly as well with pizza.

Beer cures the common cold. This was proved in a recent experiment in which scientists placed two groups of cold sufferers in a bowling alley. One group was given all the beer it could drink, while the other group was given only water. After two or three weeks, the beer drinkers exhibited no cold symptoms whatsoever, in fact couldn't even stand up, whereas the water drinkers had all gone home.

The obvious and fair solution to the housework problem is to let men do the housework for, say, the next six thousand years, to even things up. The trouble is that men, over the years, have developed an inflated notion of the importance of everything they do, so that before long they would turn housework into just as much of a charade as business is now. They would hire secretaries and buy computers and fly off to housework conferences in Bermuda, but they'd never clean anything.

• • •

In terms of sharing the housework burden, having a man around is like having a 197-pound lint ball permanently bonded to the sofa, operating the TV remote control, and periodically generating dirty underwear.

TV commercials for housework-type products are always aimed at women. We need commercials that would make housework appealing to guys. For example, there could be one where a guy opens up his refrigerator and sees ... the Swedish Bikini Team! They're trapped. Their feet are stuck in the dense brown goo that formed when barbecue sauce spilled onto the hydrator! So the guy grabs some Pine-Sol and uses its exclusive grease-cutting formula to rescue the Bikini Team members, who gather around him and express their gratitude by leaning over a lot.

On those rare occasions when a man does attempt to help out with some household responsibility, such as getting the kids dressed for school, he often discovers that his wife has established a lot of picky, technical rules, and if he doesn't do everything exactly right, he gets corrected, until finally he just gets fed up. "Wait a minute," he snaps. "Are you telling me that they have to wear shoes *every single day?*" And then he stomps off and tries to calm himself down by gripping his putter.

Some people think the way to avoid colds is to eat a lot of vitamin C, something on the order of nine billion pentagrams a day. My approach is to drink large quantities of beer. It seems to work. Since I started drinking large quantities of beer, I have not had one cold that I remember clearly.

• • •

I have seen women walk right past a TV set with a football game on and—this always amazes me—not stop to watch, even if the TV is showing replays of what we call a "good hit," which is a tackle that causes at least one major internal organ to actually fly out of a player's body.

It's that time of year when we put the holiday season behind us; a time when we suck in our stomachs, leave the cozy confines of our homes, go back out into the working world, purchase some beer, return to our homes, lie down in front of our TVs, and let our stomachs protrude back out. It's time for the pro-football playoffs.

If a guy's wife secretly throws a veteran pair of his underwear away, the guy will sense that something is wrong, and he'll whistle in a distinctive manner, and his underwear will leap out of the garbage and bound toward him like a loyal retriever. That's how close the guy-underwear bond is.

• • •

Males have a lot of trouble *not* looking at breasts. What is worse, males cannot look at breasts and think at the same time. In fact, scientists now believe that the primary biological function of breasts is to make males stupid.

One night in 1879 at a bar in a town called Menlo Park, New Jersey, some men were drinking beer, when suddenly one of them announced that he was going to invent an electric light. The others laughed, but that man got up, put on his coat and hat, and accidentally walked into the fireplace, thereby setting his coat on fire. This gave Thomas Edison, who was at another table drinking coffee, the idea of using carbonized cotton as the filament in his light bulb. So we see that beer, if used correctly, can be a tremendous force for good.

What kind of a guy is Johnny Bench, you ask? I would say, based on the time we spent together, which was in a breakfast-buffet line, that he is the kind of guy who helps himself to a croissant. This surprised me. You don't expect this from a power hitter. In fact, one of the worst insults that big-league ball players will yell at an opposing batter is "HEY (batter's name)! YOU EAT CROISSANTS!"

Most men go through life believing that they have all the clothes they will ever need. They are *extremely* suspicious of new clothes. If you give a man a tie, he will *pretend* to like it—he might even put it on—but in fact he will be very upset, because he has gone for years without this new tie, he has never felt any real need for it, and now suddenly he has to *deal* with it every time he gets ready for work.

Why do we shave? It doesn't seem like a natural activity. There are no examples of shaving in nature. The only creature that comes close is the male South Pacific Groping Beetle, which sometimes, just before mating, will slap on a little Aqua Velva. But we think this resulted from atomic testing.

came from the all-male college environment, where a person's standing in the community was judged on the basis of such factors as:

- Was he basically a good guy?
- Would he let you borrow his car?
- Would he still be basically a good guy if you or your date threw up in his car?

• • •

Imagine what will happen to this nation if large numbers of American women start using the Wonderbra. It will be catastrophic. The male half of the population will be nothing but mindless drooling Zombies of Lust. Granted, this is also true now, but it will be even worse.

Women stand just outside of the changing area, peering in, trying to get Pant News updates from their husbands:

Woman: Michael? How do they fit?

Man: They fit fine.

Woman: Michael, I want to see them.

Man: I said they fit fine.

Woman *(barging into the changing area, causing guys in there to scurry, ratlike, around their booths, attempting to cover themselves with shopping bags):* LET ME SEE THEM.

Women do not see color the way men do. If a woman tells a man she wants a green scarf, he will go out and buy what he believes to be a green scarf, based on his concept of "green," which he learned from crayons in the second grade. She will look at the scarf and see many, many colors in it, but never green. She will show it to her friends and say, "I asked Harold for a *green* scarf and just *look* what he gave to me." She and her friends will laugh about this for *years*.

A team of leading male psychological researchers at Yale deliberately looked at photographs of breasts every day for two years, at the end of which they concluded that they had failed to take any notes.

"We forgot," they said. "We'll have to do it over."

•   •   •

You have to be a real stud hombre cybermuffin to handle Windows. I have spent countless hours trying to get my computer to perform even the most basic data-processing functions, such as letting me play "F-117A Stealth Fighter" on it.

Women shave for the same reason that they wear makeup and walk around in shoes designed by Nazi medical researchers. They've been brainwashed into believing that if they don't shave, other women will snicker at them, and the only males who will be attracted to them will be members of the gorilla and tarantula families. This is nonsense. There are many cultures in which women do not shave their legs or their armpits, and, speaking as a man, let me say that I find many of these women to be exceedingly attractive, under certain lighting conditions.

was surprised to note that the Essentials catalog does not include underwear, which most guys I know view as an essential clothing item, both for formal occasions and for mopping up beer spills.

Humanity's first shaving commercial occurred when a man named Gillette got up and showed the other men that if they scraped a sharpened stone across their beards, they could tear out chunks of hair and flesh. This seemed pretty masculine to everybody, so all the men purchased sharpened stones, which immediately became obsolete when Gillette introduced a startling new shaving advance: *two* sharpened stones.

I love to watch football on TV, and I will tell you exactly why: I have no idea. Perhaps the appeal of this violent game stems from some basic biological urge that guys have, dating back millions of years to when primitive spear-carrying men would go into the forest to hunt game for their families, and their very survival depended on their ability to operate a remote control.

Every Thanksgiving, my family attends a gathering at the home of our friends Gene Weingarten and Arlene Reidy. The women all gather in one room and talk about careers, relationships, world events, etc., while the guys, most of whom see each other only once a year, all gather in front of the TV and stare, cowlike, at the football game. We even watch the pickup-truck commercials, despite the fact that most of us are journalists who rarely haul any payload larger than, say, a bagel.

I think your best bet is to give women little bottles of liquids, which are available at cosmetics counters. They have names like "Endless Night of Heavy Petting" and "Sidelong Glance" and "Eau de Water," but they all smell pretty much the same.

Your best gift bets for men are:

- Anything that needs a lot of batteries and has a lot of instructions.
- Anything that says "Ages Six to Adult" on the box.
- Anything that goes very fast and makes loud noises.

If you want to give a man something practical, consider tires. More than once I would gladly have traded all the gifts I've ever been given for a new set of tires.

A while back I wrote a column in which I was mildly critical of classical music on the grounds that it sucks and I hate it. Rather than respond to these arguments on their intellectual merits, many classical-music fans responded with snotty personal attacks in which they suggested that I am the kind of cultural moron who sits around all day watching TV with a beer in one hand and the remote control in the other. This is a lie. Sometimes I have beers in *both* hands, forcing me to operate the remote control with my feet.

If a guy is really enjoying a movie, he will not manifest this by crying; he will manifest this by chewing his Milk Duds in a more thoughtful manner.

● ● ●

As a rule, guys don't care for movies with a lot of dialogue. Guys become bored if a movie character speaks more than two consecutive sentences without some kind of important plot development, defined as shooting, punching, explosions, aliens, car chases, or Sharon Stone recrossing her legs.

According to a recent sex survey, only about 19 percent of women said they think about sex on a daily basis. So the question is, if the other 81 percent aren't thinking about sex, what *are* they thinking about? I've discussed this question with some guys I know, and the only topic we could come up with is sports. We figure that when women get together in those so-called women's groups, they're actually running fantasy-football leagues, and the reason they don't invite us is they know we'd never remember when it was our turn to bring refreshments.

Men are genetically programmed to select ugly clothing. This dates back millions of years to when primitive tribal men, responsible for defending their territory, would deck themselves out in face paint, animal heads, and nose bones, so as to look really hideous and scare off enemy tribes. If some prehistoric tribal warriors had some-how got hold of modern golf clothing, they would have ruled the rain forest.

Dressing Tip for Men: If you're going to be wearing just your underwear, you should always tuck your undershirt way down into your underpants. This is the "look" favored by the confident, sharp-dressing men found in the underwear section of the now-defunct Sears catalog, who are often depicted standing around in Rotary Club–like groups, looking relaxed and smiling, as if to say, "Our undershirts are tucked way down into our underpants, and we could not feel better about them."

Komputer Korner

Q. Which model of computer should I get?

A. The best computer for your specific needs is the one that will come on the market immediately after you actually purchase some other model. This is the key to computer ownership: There is always a newer, swoopier one coming out, and you need it. That is why we here at Komputer Korner have owned a series of progressively advanced computers, including 286s, 386s, 486s, and Pentium IIIs.

Q. What do those numbers measure?

A. Our manhood.

We do not wish to single out any specific gender here, but a lot of men *never* take their caps off—not in restaurants, not at funerals, not in bed, not while undergoing brain surgery. And even if you *do* get the owner to remove the cap, you find that it's encrusted with a thick layer of grime that has been formed into a kind of mortar by dried sweat. This poses a real cleaning problem, and until recently the only proven way to solve it was to make a paste mixture of baking soda and kerosene, rub it thoroughly into the cap, and set fire to it.

Aside from the vision thing and the weight thing and the need to take an afternoon nap almost immediately after I wake up and the fact that random hairs (I'm talking about long hairs, the kind normally associated with Cher) occasionally erupt from deep inside my ears—aside from these minor problems, I am a superb physical specimen easily mistaken for Brad Pitt.

Males, as a group, have the fashion sense of cement. Oh, I realize that there are exceptions—men who know how to pick your elegant suits and perfectly color-coordinated accessories. But for every man walking around looking tasteful, there are at least ten men walking around wearing orange plaid Bermuda shorts with nonmatching boxer shorts sticking out above *and* below, and sometimes also poking out through the fly.

Other than being functionally blind at close range, I remain in superb physical condition for a man of my age who can no longer fit into any of his pants. I have definitely been gaining some weight in the midriff region, despite a rigorous diet regimen of drinking absolutely no beer whatsoever after I pass out.

A big problem is that men and women often do not agree on what is boring. Men can devote an entire working week to discussing a single pass-interference penalty; women find this boring, yet can be fascinated by a four-hour movie with subtitles wherein the entire plot consists of a man and a woman yearning to have, but never actually having, a relationship. Men *hate* that. Men can take maybe forty-five seconds of yearning, and then they want everybody to get naked. Followed by a car chase. A movie called *Naked People in Car Chases* would do really well among men.

To learn more about the current men's fashion scene, get a copy of *Esquire* and *GQ* and study the ads and articles presenting the latest styles, making a mental note to never, ever wear any of them, because unless you're a male model, you'd look stupid. Just wear a regular blue suit like everybody else and try to have both shoes the same color.

Women constantly complain about guys changing the channels, as though guys do this for no reason. In fact, a guy clicking a remote control is obeying an ancient "hunter-gatherer" instinct—an instinct that has compelled guys ever since the Stone Age to keep searching, searching, searching, in a ceaseless quest to benefit the tribal unit by locating a mastodon, which could be used for food, or by monitoring the show *Baywatch*.

Some people—and when I say "some people," I mean "women"—complain that guys spit too much. A guy will be in a public place such as a city street or baseball game or wedding reception, and he'll suddenly rear back and launch what the medical profession refers to as a "loogie," and some people will say: "EWWWW! Gross!"

The *University of Washington Daily* published a report headlined "Fraternity Game Turns Into Arrest." According to this report, guys were on the roof of the Theta Delta Chi fraternity house, and, as guys will do when they spend time together in an elevated location, they began sharing their innermost feelings.

I am of course kidding. These guys, being guys, began dropping things off the roof, starting with smaller items, and escalating to a chair and a rowing machine. Far be it from me to indulge in sex stereotyping, but I'm willing to bet that the reaction of readers to this story is divided along gender lines:

Female Reaction: "Why would anybody do anything so *stupid*?"

Male Reaction: "A rowing machine! *Cool!*"

A Harris survey was released showing that 70 percent of American men do not view birth control as their responsibility. This resulted in the usual round of male-bashing by the usual critics, who as usual failed to note the many areas in which men take on *more* than their fair share of responsibility, such as spider killing, channel changing, referee critiquing, scratching, and traffic gestures.

If you were standing in the middle of a bridge spanning a wilderness gorge, at the bottom of which was a spectacular white-water river, what would you do?

Female Response: Admire the view.

Male Response: Spit.

Yes, there are few things that a guy enjoys more than proudly watching a gob of spit falling a tremendous distance. This is a male impulse that females cannot relate to, just as males cannot relate to the female impulse to go into greeting-card stores and spend hours shopping for greeting cards even when there is no particular occasion or person you need to send a greeting card to, which is what women frequently do when guys are out spitting.

With spring upon us, you may find yourself near a woman in the throes of planning a wedding; if so, you need to recognize that she is under severe pressure, and above all you need to do exactly as she says. If she wants you to wrap yourself in toilet paper, or purchase and wear a bridesmaid's dress that makes you look like a walking Barcalounger, *just do it*. You should do it even if you are the groom.

In my era, the TV Superman, who was more powerful than a locomotive, did not have visible stomach muscles. In fact, he didn't have much muscle definition at all; he pretty much looked like a middle-aged guy at a Halloween party wearing a Superman costume made from pajamas, a guy who had definitely put in some time around the onion dip. From certain angles he looked as though he *weighed* more than a locomotive. But he got the job done. He was always flying to crime scenes faster than a speeding bullet in a horizontal position with his arms out in front of him.

Study Question: Did he fly in this position because he *had* to? Or was it that the public would have been less impressed if he had flown in a sitting position, like an airline passenger, reading a magazine and eating honey-roasted peanuts?

As a boy, I was into baseball. My friends and I collected baseball cards, the kind that came in a little pack with a dusty, pale-pink rectangle of linoleum-textured World War II surplus bubble gum that was far less edible than the cards themselves. Like every other male my age who collected baseball cards as a boy, I now firmly believe that at one time I had the original rookie cards of Mickey Mantle, Jackie Robinson, Ty Cobb, Babe Ruth, Jim Thorpe, Daniel Boone, Goliath, etc., and that I'd be able to sell my collection for $163 million today except my mom threw it out.

While the bride has many responsibilities at the wedding, the groom has many responsibilities, too. According to ancient tradition, on the morning of the wedding the groom must check the TV listings to make sure that there is no playoff game scheduled during the ceremony because if there is, he would have to miss it (the ceremony).

I was very relieved to find out about a University of Pennsylvania study which found that, as males get older, their brains shrink and that this was not just my personal problem, but a problem afflicting the brains of males in general, although, as a frequent flier, I hope it doesn't extend to male airplane pilots ("Ladies and gentlemen, we are approaching either Pittsburgh or Honolulu, so at this time I'm going to push the button that either illuminates the fasten-seat belt signs or shuts off all the engines").

I hate male swimmers and divers, who, in addition to being Greek gods, wear ridiculously tiny "Speedo"-style bathing suits that are approximately the size of a contact lens. I bet if you went into the locker room, you'd see swimmers on hands and knees, peering at the floor, going, "I lost my suit!"

I myself wear a style of bathing suit known as "trunks." This style has an important safety feature: When you jump into the water feet-first, your suit develops pontoon-size air bags, which keep you afloat. Material from a single pair of my trunks could supply the Speedo needs of Olympic swimmers through the next five Summer Games.

At Camp Sharparoon, I used to lead a party of boys ages ten and eleven into the uncharted wilderness around Dover Furnace, New York, aware we would have to survive for an entire night with nothing to sustain us except roughly two hundred pounds of marshmallows, graham crackers, and Hershey bars. We used these to make "s'mores." Sometimes we'd hook up with girl campers and make "s'mores" together; this is when I observed a fundamental difference between boys and girls:

How Girls Make "S'mores"—(1) Place Hershey bars on graham crackers. (2) Toast marshmallows. (3) Place toasted marshmallows on Hershey bars to melt chocolate.

How Boys Make "S'mores"—(1) Eat Hershey bars. (2) Eat marshmallows. (3) Throw graham crackers at other boys.

The brain-shrinkage study, which found that, as males get older, their brains shrink, makes me feel a lot better, because now I know that I'm not getting stupid alone; billions of guys are getting stupid with me, as evidenced by:

- Golf
- Comb-overs
- The U.S. Senate
- Marlon Brando

I think Older Male Brain Shrinkage (OMBS) should be recognized as a disability by the government. At the least, we should have a law requiring everyone to wear a name tag. Older males would be exempt from this requirement, because they wouldn't be able to find their tags. I have many other strong views on this subject, but I can't remember what they are.

I think that for an activity to qualify as being an Olympic sport, it must meet the strict criterion of being some activity that I, personally, used to have to do in gym class. By this criterion, there would be no Team Handball, nor would there be Air Pistol, nor would there be any of those sports that sound like prescription drugs, such as Heptathlon. These would be replaced by traditional gym-class sports such as Dodge Ball, the Dreaded Rope Climb, the Squat Thrust, the Men's Towel Snap, and Spud.

I am crazy mad in love with the hunting community. This is because hunters, in their neverending quest for new and better ways to outwit woodland creatures with the intelligence of chewing gum, have created a market for all kinds of wonderful products. Urine, for example. I am deadly serious. Look through any hunting-supplies catalog, and you will find a variety of fine deer urines for sale. Hunters sprinkle the urine around to attract deer, which the hunters can then shoot in a sportsmanlike fashion.

The state of Montana (Official Motto: "Moo") announced there would be no speed limit during daylight hours. I am not a legal scholar, but to me "no speed limit" means that, theoretically, you can go four hundred miles per hour, right?

If that were true, Montana would become a popular destination for your average guy driver on vacation with his family because guys like to cover a tremendous amount of ground. A guy in Vacation Driving Mode prefers not to stop the car at all except in the case of a bursting appendix, and even then he's likely to say, "Can you hold it a little longer? We're only 157 miles from Leech World!"

My dad wore one of those Russian-style hats that were semipopular with middle-aged guys in the early '60s. The fur on his was dark and curly; it looked as though this hat had been made from a poodle. My dad was the smartest, most decent, most perceptive person I've ever known, but he was a card-carrying member of the Fashion Club for Men Who Wear Bermuda Shorts with the Waist Up Around Their Armpits, Not to Mention Sandals with Dark Socks.

You know the Budweiser holiday TV commercial, the one wherein the famous Budweiser Clydesdales are pulling a sleigh, clip-clopping along a snow-covered road at dusk and winding up at a cozy house? Did you ever wonder what that sleigh is carrying? Beer. The occupants of that cozy house are going to toss down brewskis, then take the Clydesdales for a joyride and see what those babies can do on the interstate.

Fact: Eighty-three percent of accidents involving tractor-trailers and sleighs occur during the holidays. We are not being critical. We think that, except for making a beverage that tastes like carbonated pig drool, Budweiser is a fine organization.

believe that, in general, women are saner than men.

For example: If you see people who have paid good money to stand in an outdoor stadium on a freezing December day wearing nothing on the upper halves of their bodies except paint, those people will be male.

Without males, there would be no such sport as professional lawn mower racing.

Also, there would be a 100 percent decline in the annual number of deaths related to efforts to shoot beer cans off of heads.

There would also be no such words as "wedgie" and "noogie."

Auto racing drivers are—and I means this in a positive way—insane. They strap themselves into extremely powerful, cramped, hot, loud, stripped-down cars without even a rudimentary CD player; then they spend hours screaming around a racetrack bumper to bumper, going so fast that you expect them at any moment to hit Warp Speed and vanish altogether into a *Star Trek* episode. When they crash—which they all do, sooner or later—they soup up their wheel-chair motors and try to heal as fast as possible so they can race *again*.

Men tend to feel positive about their hair. Even if a man has a grand total of only four hairs left, he will grow them to the length of extension cords and carefully arrange them so they are running exactly parallel, two inches apart, across his otherwise stark naked skull, and he will look at himself and think, "Whoa, these four hairs are looking *good*."

Most men do not spend a lot of time fretting about the size of their pants. Many men wear jeans with the size printed right on the back label, so that if you're standing behind a man in a supermarket line, you can read his waist and inseam size. A man could have, say, a fifty-two-inch waist and a thirty-inch inseam, and his label will proudly display this information, which is basically the same thing as having a sign that says: "Howdy! My butt is the size of a Federal Express truck!"

The coolest thing about "Louie Louie" was I could play it on the guitar. When I became part of a band in a futile attempt to appeal to girls, "Louie Louie" was the first song I learned. Our band would whomp on our cheap guitars plugged into our amplifiers, and our dogs would hide and our moms would leave the house on unnecessary errands, and we'd wail into our fast-food-drive-thru-intercom-quality public-address system, and when the last out-of-tune notes leaked from the room, we'd look at each other and say "Hey! We sound like the Kingsmen!" The beauty was, we kind of *did*.

When I went to trade in my sport utility vehicle, I was going to buy another practical car. But I ran into a salesperson named Jerry. Jerry's former profession was—really—powerboat racer. In addition to selling cars, he is coproducing a kickboxing movie. So in terms of practicality, Jerry is not Mr. Both Feet on the Ground. If he could have, I think he would have sold me an F-16 ("Dave, if you're willing to do business today, we're going to throw in the floor mats *and* the heat-seeking missile package").

I warn you: If you go to the U.S. Open tennis tournament, you might be intimidated by the crowd. I was. I'm more used to football crowds, the type of crowd where you can paint your body and dance on the seats and blow on a giant plastic horn and wear an animal-shaped hat the size of a fire hydrant and scream insults at the officials so loud that traces of your saliva wind up in the hair of people sitting thirty-eight rows in front of you, and you will not even be noticed.

Whether you're a woman or a man, you should know the basics of hairstyle management, as presented here in the popular Q-and-A format:

Q. Should balding white men shave their heads, the way many African American men, such as Michael Jordan, do?

A. No. It's not fair, but the simple truth is that balding African American men look cool when they shave their heads, whereas balding white men look like giant thumbs.

I've reported on the sport of snowplow hockey, in which guys driving trucks use snowplow blades to knock a bowling ball past trucks driven by opposing guys. This is not to be confused with car bowling, in which guys in airplanes try to drop bowling balls onto cars. I've also reported on guys going off a ski jump in a canoe, and guys trying to build a modernized version of a catapultlike weapon, then using it to hurl a Buick two hundred yards.

These are guy activities, activities that, when you describe them to both males and females, provoke two very different reactions:

Male Reaction: "Cool!"

Female Reaction: *"Why?"*

I got a call from a guy I know named Carl. "I think I want to buy an electric guitar," he said.

At some point or another, almost every guy wants an electric guitar. It would not surprise me to learn that late at night, in the Vatican, the pope picks one up and plays "Hang On, Sloopy." Electric guitars exert a strong appeal for guys, because they combine two critical elements:

1. A guitar.

2. Electricity.

Taken separately, these elements have little intrinsic value. But combined, they have an almost magical effect: They enable a mediocre guitar player, or even a bad guitar player, to play *way* louder.

If you're a man, at some point a woman will ask you how she looks. "How do I look?" she'll ask.

You must be careful how you answer this question. The best technique is to form an honest yet sensitive opinion, then collapse on the floor with some kind of fatal seizure. Trust me, this is the easiest way out. Because you will never come up with the right answer.

Women generally do not think of their looks in the same way that men do. Most men form an opinion of how they look in seventh grade, and they stick to it for the rest of their lives. Some men form the opinion that they are irresistible stud muffins, and they do not change this opinion even when their faces sag and their noses bloat to the size of eggplants and their eyebrows grow together to form what appears to be a giant forehead-dwelling caterpillar.

Most men think of themselves as average looking. Being average does not bother them; average is fine, for men. This is why men never ask anybody how they look. Their primary form of beauty care is to shave themselves, which is essentially the same form of beauty care that they give to their lawns. If, at the end of his four-minute daily beauty regimen, a man has managed to wipe most of the shaving cream out of his hair and is not bleeding too badly, he feels he has done all he can, so he stops thinking about his appearance and devotes his mind to more critical issues, such as the Super Bowl.

Most women are very sensitive to odors, whereas men, largely as a result of smelling their own selves over the eons, have reached the point where they tend not to detect any aroma below the level of a municipal dump. That's the way it is in my household. Five times per week, my wife and I have the same conversation. Michelle says, "What's that smell?" And I say, "What smell?" And she looks at me as though I am demented and says, "You can't *smell* that?"

The truth is there could be a stack of truck tires burning in the living room, and I wouldn't necessarily smell it. Whereas Michelle can detect a lone spoiled grape two houses away.

For years women have made fun of men for refusing to ask directions. But did it ever occur to you women that we men have a *reason?* Did it ever occur to you that we might be thinking about something that *you don't know?* That something is this: Under the Rules of Guy Conduct, if you're a guy driving a car, and you don't know how to get where you're going, and you pull over to ask another guy, and he *does* know, then he is legally entitled to *take your woman!* Yes! He can

 just lean through the window and grab her! I bet you feel silly now!

I once saw an *Oprah* show wherein supermodel Cindy Crawford dispensed makeup tips to the studio audience. Cindy had these middle-aged women applying beauty products to their faces, even though, no matter how carefully they applied these products, they would never look like Cindy Crawford.

You will never get middle-aged men to sit in a room and apply cosmetics under the instruction of Brad Pitt, in hopes of looking more like him. Men would realize this task was pointless and demeaning. They would find some way to bolster their self-esteem that did not require looking like Brad Pitt. They would say to Brad: "Oh *yeah?* Well, what do you know about *lawn care,* pretty boy?"

Guys generally like to find a recipe that works for them and stick with it. For example, I know a sportswriter named Bob who, to my knowledge, has never in his life cooked anything except Stouffer's frozen French bread pizza. This is all he has in his freezer. If he hosted a Thanksgiving dinner, he'd serve a large Stouffer's French bread pizza, stuffed with smaller Stouffer's French bread pizzas. At the Stouffer's factory, they probably have a whole department devoted exclusively to Bob, called "the Department of Bob," which monitors Bob's pizza consumption and has a fleet of loaded resupply trucks ready to roll when he runs low.

If you are planning to host a Super Bowl party, you should get the old standby—potato chips—but you should also, for nutritional balance, put out a bowl of carrot sticks. If you have no carrot sticks, you can use pine cones or used electrical fuses, because nobody will eat them anyway. This is no time for nutritional balance: This is the Super Bowl, for God's sake.

A commonly held (by women) negative stereotype about guys of the male gender is that they cannot find things around the house, especially things in the kitchen.

I could respond to this stereotype in a snide manner by making generalizations about women. I could point out that, to judge from the covers of countless women's magazines, the two topics most interesting to women are (1) Why men are all disgusting pigs, and (2) How to attract men.

grant that it is not easy being a female, and
I realize there are certain hardships that only
females must endure, such as childbirth, waiting
in lines for public rest room stalls, and a crip-
pling, psychotic obsession with shoe color. Also,
females tend to reach emotional maturity very
quickly, so that by age seven they are no longer
capable of seeing the humor in loud inadvertent
public blasts of flatulence, whereas males can
continue to derive vast enjoyment from this well
into their eighties.

What this nation needs is an Institute of Guy Domestic Research, where guy scientists wearing white laboratory coats stained with Cheez Whiz would conduct experiments to answer household questions that concern guys, such as: If you leave your used underwear in the freezer for a week, is that as good as laundering it? Or should you also splash a little Old Spice on it, just to be safe?

Guys are sometimes accused of not having a domestic "flair" just because they tend to accessorize a room with used pizza boxes. But there are examples of guys coming up with decorative "touches" that Martha Stewart would never conceive of even with the aid of world-class narcotics.

So let's not say that guys are not domestic. When we see a guy who makes drapes by nailing trash bags over his windows, let's remember that he might have a legitimate domestic reason, such as that he ran out of duct tape.

Nature has given males the heaviest burden of all: the burden of always having to Make the First Move, and thereby risk getting Shot Down. It's true throughout the animal kingdom. If you watch nature shows, you'll note that whatever species they are talking about—birds, crabs, spiders, clams—it is *always* the male who has to take the initiative. It's always the male bird who does the courting dance, making a total moron of himself, while the female bird just stands there, looking aloof, thinking about what she's going to tell her girlfriends. ("And then he hopped around on one foot! Like I'm supposed to be impressed by *that!*")

Women have an awesome power over men, and I hope you women understand this. Women, I hope that the next time a guy walks up and uses some incredibly lame, boneheaded line on you, you will remember that he is under the intense pressure of wanting to impress you enough so that you might want to get to know him better and maybe eventually, perhaps within the next fifteen minutes, mate with him, thereby enabling the survival of the human race, which believe me is the only thing that we males are truly concerned about.

What explains the appeal of the *Star Wars* series? Speaking as one who saw *Return of the Jedi* on video at least fourteen thousand times when my son was four, I would say that the key element is the theme of Good versus Evil. Good is of course represented by Luke Skywalker (Mark Hamill), who has the Force, a mystical, universal power that causes him to be attracted to his sister. Fortunately, Luke gets over that and meets a wise Jedi master named Yoda (Raymond Burr) who trains Luke to harness the awesome power of the Force so that he can speak lines of really bad dialogue without laughing.

When I was maybe six years old, I spent many hours on a dirt pile next to my house, making roads and stuff with toy trucks and bulldozers. This was hard work, because in addition to pushing the heavy equipment around, I had to make the motor noise with my mouth—*brrrmmmm*—for hours on end, keeping a fine mist of spit raining down on the construction site. Almost all boys do this, yet for some reason most of us, when we grow up, rarely operate any piece of equipment more impressive than hedge trimmers.

Actual football fans are the kind of guys who paint their bodies in their team colors and show up at the stadium at 6 A.M. and spend the next twelve hours drinking fifty-three beers and shouting "WHOOOO" and sometimes accidentally setting their hair on fire. And they don't do this just on game days, either: Your true fan does this *every day of the week.*

In an effort to calm her husband when they are late for a party, a wife may call out the words that cause despair in the hearts of men: "I'm almost ready! I'm just putting on my makeup!"

To the husband, these two statements contradict each other. It's like saying "I'm very short! I'm thirty-eight feet tall!" or "You can believe me! I'm Bill Clinton!" because to the husband, "I'm just putting on my makeup" means "I'm painstakingly applying 450 coats of beauty products to my face using an applicator the width of a human hair."

Oh, I could make snide generalizations about women. I could ask why a woman would walk up to a perfectly innocent man who is minding his own business watching basketball and demand to know if a certain pair of pants makes her butt look too big, and then, no matter what he answers, get mad at him.

• • •

Women often ask, "What do men *really* want, deep in their souls?" The best answer—based on in-depth analysis of the complex and subtle interplay of thought, instinct, and emotion that constitutes the male psyche—is that deep in their souls, men want to watch stuff go "bang."